gōl

a curated guide for the modern day job hunt

KATHY ENGEN
& LINDA HEATH

ISBN 13: 978-163489041

Library of Congress Catalog Number: 2016941502
Printed in the United States of America
First Printing: 2016
20 19 18 17 16   5 4 3 2 1

COVER AND INTERIOR DESIGN BY JESS MORPHEW

Wise Ink Creative Publishing
Minneapolis, MN 55431
www.wiseinkpub.com

To order, visit www.shiftandspark.com,
www.SeattleBookCompany.com, or call (734) 426-6248.
Wholesaler and reseller discounts available.

dedication

*We did it, and we couldn't
have done it without you.
Thank you for your
patience and support.*

Peter, Alexander, McKinley,
&
Matt, Preston, and Dillon.

contents

introduction *9*

Goal

/gōl/

noun

The object
of a person's
ambition or
effort;
an aim or
desired result.

introduction

et's be honest: finding a job is not an easy task. You may not have a job because it was recently eliminated, or your job may be fine but uninspiring and so you've been thinking about looking for other opportunities, but life has gotten in the way.

No matter how you slice it, there comes a time in life when you need to find something new. Unfortunately, the path to the next job isn't always clear. Where do you start? Luckily for you, we've been there; with Kathy's experience in mentoring and empowering job seekers and Linda's experience in being "restructured," we gained wisdom and insight on the big picture. Along the way, we also gleaned advice from brilliant minds willing to share how they architected their search.

Bringing these ideas to life was another story. Collected in an orange Russell+Hazel® binder (gotta have something nice to look at when you're on your search), these ideas were filed away in the basement after Linda's job search. During a particularly liberating 'Tini Tuesday happy hour with a group of like-minded professionals, the idea came to us that maybe this packet full of ideas could be shared—as a book for the benefit of job seekers everywhere. Our goal was to meet every week, and we did for a year and a half—culling through ideas, LinkedIn, résumés, and dress codes. Slowly, these separate ideas came together to form a pattern, and our goal of bringing *Gōl* to life started to take shape. Then we shared and tested the ideas with our friends to validate whether it could actually help them reach their goals. Several "wine clicks" later (writing and researching while drinking wine—highly recommended for job searchers) what resulted from that fateful happy hour is the book you hold in your hands.

As we've said before, finding a job is not an easy task; it takes time and a lot of effort to be successful, and without a roadmap, many of us lose our motivation and ultimately lose our way. So let *Gōl* be your roadmap to help you dig deep and identify the career path that is best for you right now and help you maintain your motivation to achieve your next step. This book will provide the framework you need to create a plan and the perspective you need to turn that plan into action. To navigate through our book, think of it as a set of modules, each chapter specifically created to build on the last. It takes you through the journey from your initial job search to employment. With each chapter, you'll find a little genuine advice with an activity to help you think through and internalize where you want to go. These activities will help you crystallize your personal and professional goals and connect you to the right people at the right companies. While there's no job guarantee—it's still your job to find a job—*Gōl* will give your job search structure and purpose.

As you embark on your adventure, here's a little reminder from fellow author Gayle Harper's book *Roadtrip with a Raindrop*:

"Life is meant to be easy. We tend to make it much harder than it needs to be with all the requirements that it go the way we think it ought to. When we can just go with it, like the river does, then we find out usually that the way life unfolds is much better than the way we imagined that it should."

"The future depends on what you do today."

–Mahatma Gandhi

chapter 1

Tomorrow Starts Today

etting a jump on tomorrow is simply reflecting on what's happening this very moment and what you would like to have happen instead. This also means being honest with yourself about whether you're genuinely happy with the career path you've chosen thus far. Because at the end of the day, it's you who has to walk the trails, and there's nothing worse than making it halfway there only to realize you brought heels when you really needed a pair of flats to make it to your destination.

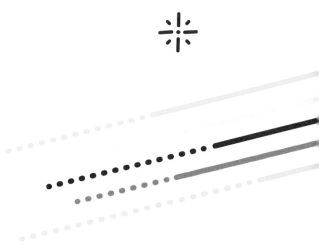

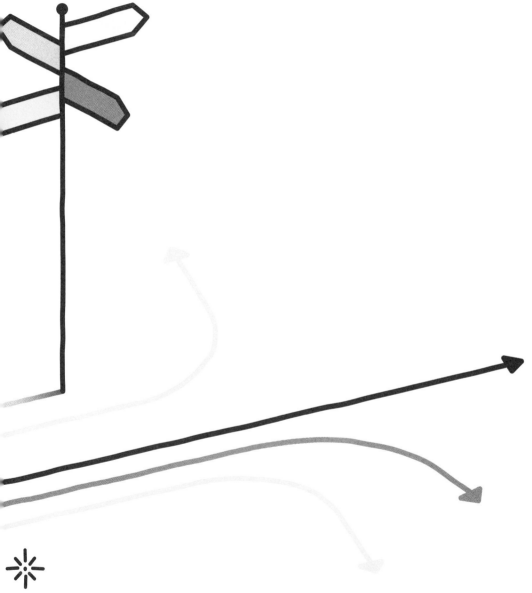

To get in the right frame of mind, start by identifying at least three things that are happening in your life right now. Yes, the good, the bad, and the ugly. Yours can be all good, all ugly, or somewhere in between; jot a few of them down.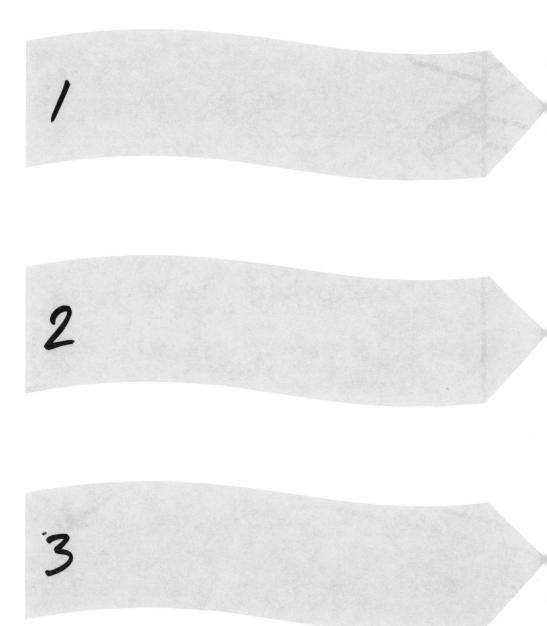

1

2

3

Now where do you want to go? You got it—write it here.

1

2

3

If you're a visual, creative person, it may be easier for you to create a vision board of where you want to go instead of writing it down. To create a vision board, start by collecting beautiful images and

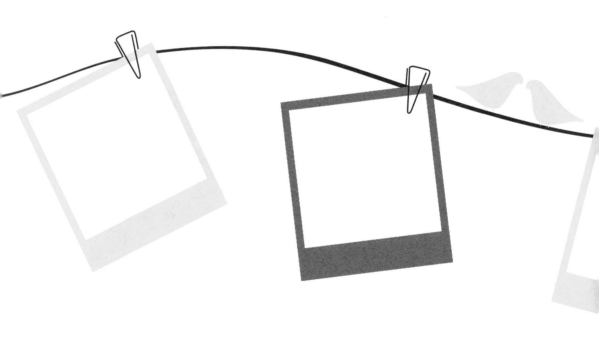

inspiring quotes you find that appeal to you and demand your focus. Then gather them all in one spot. This is easily achieved with poster board or online using Pinterest.

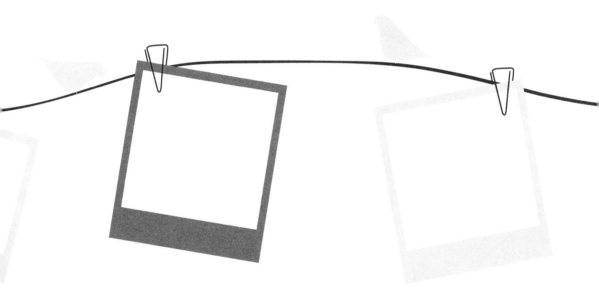

However, getting started isn't enough to keep going. You need the right shoes, the right people, and the right plan. In other words, you need goals!

"We have to continually be jumping off cliffs and developing our wings on the way down."

—Kurt Vonnegut

chapter 2

Ready, Set, Gōl

To help you stay focused and moving forward with your job search, take the time at the beginning of your journey to define your professional goals and your personal goals. It gives you a North Star, a way to measure what you are accomplishing. And how does this fit into your job search? Use your goals as a gut check against a job description, future boss, etc. If one of your personal goals is to have a more balanced life and a job description reads that travel is required seventy-five percent of the time, this is definitely something you'll want to ask about when you are interviewing (or possibly takes the job off your list altogether).

You're probably thinking, *Why two sets of goals?* Here's why: it is important to realize that your goals may or may not complement each other, and you will need to be able to distinguish between the two types. Two things happened with this section of the book when we shared it with our gang for their thoughts. First, many had a similar reaction: "It never occurred to me to take the time to write down my personal goals." They had been so focused on their career journeys that the "me" part fell away, overshadowed with life's other responsibilities. One friend shared that as she took the time to think about her life, accomplishments, and where she wanted to be personally, it ended up changing a lot of what went into her professional goals. It was an emotional experience. Second came the realization that women might not feel they can achieve both their personal and professional goals. Every year we have to revisit professional goals during annual reviews, but we might not have our own personal "How's it going?" So often we are judged by professional accomplishments, but those very accomplishments may be out of whack, as we haven't checked them against where we want to go as people.

A very successful friend working as a VP in corporate America has never missed one of her son's soccer games (that usually start between 3:30 and 4:00). She shared that, early in her career, she had a mentor who said to her, "My litmus test is: If I am on my deathbed, will I wish I had attended one more meeting or spent more time with my family?" Our friend fully embraces that spirit, so she works over lunch and may stay later on other days, but she makes it her goal to be there to see her son play. That's one point of view. What's yours?

goals may or may not complement each other

It's time for you to create your personal and professional goals. Grab a glass of wine, find a quiet place, turn on a little Sinatra or funk—whatever gets you comfortable—and look inside yourself.

You may be surprised with the valuable insights you find.

Now a word of advice: goals can be exactly what you make them. To help get a little perspective around your efforts, check that your goals pass this test. **Ask yourself:**

1 *Are my goals clearly definable?*

2 *Are my goals actionable?*

3 *Are my goals achievable within a realistic time frame?*

Let's get started:

Personal Goals

Take a moment and think about your current life as a woman, wife, mom, friend, etc., and think about what kind of personal goals would help fulfill your life and roles. Most importantly, remember that your personal goals can be as simple and as small as waking up at 5:30 a.m. to exercise every morning for a month. Of course, they can also be as big as saving up for a trip to Paris. Either way, achieving your personal goals will not only help you feel great and accomplished but will also pave the way for achieving those professional goals of yours, too.

So what's on your list? Learning to cook, actually reading the book from book club, starting a blog . . . ready, set, gōl!

Professional Goals

Now on to the professional goals. Think about the roles you've had in your work life. What motivated you? What did you love to do, and what were you really good at? And more important, what don't you like? Understanding what makes you tick (and what doesn't) can help you discover and uncover wants and needs you may not have realized.

What motivates me?

What do I love? What am I really good at?

What don't I like to do?

Then take what you've learned and turn it into your professional goals. The goals you record here will become your "plan," since they are time sensitive, they should be transferred to your calendar after you complete this activity.

Ready, set, gōl!

Now that you've generated your list of goals, go back and rank them—personal and professional. After you've slept on the list, do you still feel the same? If so, great. If not, revise them.

Remember: goals are not accomplished overnight. Most are made up of a bunch of small tasks that will lead you to the end goal. So now that they are ranked, break them down further. Make a list; this will become your to-do list for actually accomplishing your goals. It may help to start backwards from the goal. Create lists for daily, weekly, and monthly tasks that will bring you to your goal. The key is to parcel it out. When we set out to write this book, it was daunting. We had so many ideas and directions. We parceled it out by committing to meeting every week, keeping a running to-do list, and then picking five things on that to-do list to accomplish each time we met. If we didn't accomplish all five things, we gave ourselves homework to be accomplished by the following week to keep us on task. Breaking these big goals into smaller tasks made it actually doable.

Remember: goals are not accomplished overnight

Find the system that works best for you.

After you've documented your goals, share them. Share your plans, your intentions, and even your to-do list with the people who sit at your table—those special people who will support you in achieving your goals. They will hold you accountable, give you guidance, keep you focused, and celebrate with you when you achieve your aspirations.

Not exactly sure who has a seat at your table and who's just dropping by for dinner?

The next chapter will help you examine and nominate your friends and colleagues and assign seats at your table.

"The people who are happy for your happiness and sad for your sadness . . . keep them around."

— Dr. Steve Maraboli

chapter 3

Who Sits At Your Table

Before sharing your personal and professional goals with the people at your table, it's important to identify who actually has or will have a seat.

At home, the seats are reserved for family. However, the table arrangement is also a metaphor for your professional life. In your professional life, your table consists of your board of directors who coach, guide, or cheer you to greatness. And reserving those seats takes some thinking and a lot of trust.

For starters, your table doesn't have to be only people you work with professionally. These are the people who have your best interest in mind: close friends, trusted work peers, your first boss, or your boss's boss.

The key to your table arrangement is to have a trusted variety. Savvy politicians, creative problem solvers, good listeners, seasoned mentors, entrepreneurs—your table should hold different types of voices from people with varying skills and talents. Each person should have something valuable to bring to the table. Everyone should also bring intelligent and unbiased opinions to help you navigate this journey.

Some of your board members will last a lifetime; others will help you through specific and temporary situations. Continuously cultivate your table so that it works best for where you are right now.

Here are the steps to seating your table:

1   Start by brainstorming your list of trusted go-to people. Who immediately comes to mind? Then dig deeper to the not-so-obvious people. Write their names down followed by why they are on your list. Realize that not everyone on your list should make it onto your board of directors. There will be cuts, and that's okay.

name	why
name	why
name	why
name	why
name	why
name	why
name	why
name	why

2   Selectively edit the names from your master list. To help you better navigate through your list, develop a criterion for the people who belong on your board. It could be someone who brought clarity to a complicated situation or someone who patiently coached you in the past. It can be someone who will hold you accountable or someone you simply admire. Whatever it is, learn to see how each person can bring value or expertise to your daily, weekly, monthly, and big-picture goal(s).

3   Invite them to become a member of your board. Now that you've identified your key people, make meaningful connections. Share this exercise with them, and don't be afraid to ask them to be your mentor or your sounding board. Be honest with them, and explain why you want them on your board. If you need them on there simply to keep you going and hold you accountable, tell them that. Being specific about your needs will help them help you. Most importantly, keep in mind that this person is going out of their way to share their expertise and time with you. To keep them on your board, make sure you don't waste the valuable time and energy they've donated your way. Follow through and follow up with them. To give them the boost they deserve when you start hitting your milestones, random thank-you notes can go a long way.

4   Gut-check your table once a year to remind yourself of these special people and the advice, courage, and mentoring they can bring to you as your life and situations change. Then repeat this exercise to see if the individuals from the past are still relevant to the present or future.

If you think there are too many chairs around this table, you can remove one.

After the members of your board of directors have accepted your invitation, give them a place at your table. Make sure you give yourself the seat in the middle.

If you think there are too many chairs around this table, you can remove one. But don't add any; too many people gathered around a table often leads to chaos, and you don't want to get lost in the shuffle.

"I am who
I am today
because of
the choices
I made
yesterday."

–Eleanor Roosevelt

chapter 4

Slumps, Bumps, and Celebrations

L et's set an expectation for the road ahead: no matter how much you plan and define your goals, your search will have its highs and lows. Your job is to manage the emotional roller coaster that goes with each. Planning for it can actually help you. Let your plan show you the way.

The key to each slump, bump, and celebration is to acknowledge and embrace that it is happening. Because they are not only beneficial but also inevitable. Oftentimes, slumps happen right after experiencing a lot of positive activity. In other words, you may be saying, "I have more interviews lined up than pairs of shoes and still no offers." That's completely okay. Take a deep breath, give thanks for what you've learned about yourself thus far, and trust that the right job is coming. After all, what's the destination without the journey?

Then there are those out-of-the-blue bumps. Maybe the job you thought you were perfect for and told everyone about doesn't pan out. Instead of creating more bumps for yourself, acknowledge where you are and take a closer look at your skill set and how it applies to this job. If possible, ask for additional feedback, and then let go of what no longer serves you.

Slumps and bumps aside, there will also be a handful of great celebrations to clink your glass to. You may not have received that offer yet, but maybe you just got another interview with the same company or you just made a great connection with someone who works for the company you've wanted to work for. Give yourself an extended moment to take it in. Take a day off from the job hunt, go for a walk, mix yourself a celebratory cocktail, and say cheers with your favorite people.

You should be able to look to your board of directors when the time comes to pull you out of a slump, help keep you going after a bump, and be there when you just need a celebratory dose.

"Dreams don't work unless you do."

–John C. Maxwell

chapter 5

Résumé

With endless how-tos and advice, getting started on your résumé can seem like an overwhelming task. The good news? We're simplifying it here.

Tips to Get You Started (and Keep You Going)

1   **KEYWORDS:** What words are key to your industry? If you're not sure where to start, find five jobs you would like to apply for online, print them out, and highlight the consistent keywords and phrases you see in each job description. Chances are you will quickly start to notice a pattern.

2   **FOCUS ON WHAT YOU WANT TO TALK ABOUT IN THE INTERVIEW.** This will drive the content of the résumé; what have you done that you're proud of? Then tell us how you did it, and be specific about your ownership. What were the results of your work? This is really what it's all about. If you are having difficulties remembering, your annual reviews can help you remember what you did.

3   **USE THE SCOPE OF YOUR ROLE** and what attributes define it, like budget, the number of direct reports, and the level of people you interacted with (e.g., C-level). Use specifics and numbers.

4   **AVOID INTERNAL JARGON.** Abbreviations and jargon are great internally, just not anywhere throughout your résumé. Remember, just because you used a term at your company does not mean it is universal. ISM could stand for In Store Marketing, Institute for Supply Management, or I Sabotage Myself.

5   **ACTIONS SPEAK LOUDER THAN WORDS.** Action verbs are critical when describing your experience and accomplishments. Start each bullet point with a strong action verb that accurately describes what you did (e.g. managed, consulted, developed, directed, etc.). Avoid using words as generic as "worked" and "responsible," and try to keep your verbs slightly different so that your résumé doesn't sound like a robot on repeat.

Tips to Format
Your Résumé for Success

The goal here is to first and foremost get your résumé down on paper. Then you can play with the design and layout as you wish.

1 **MAKE IT EASY TO READ AND DIGEST.** You want to make it easy for the person skimming (reading if you're lucky) your résumé to find exactly what they need. This includes an easy-to-read font, such as Ariel, Helvetica, or Times New Roman. Comic Sans and Handwriting scripts are difficult to read.

2 **EMBRACE WHITE SPACE.** Never underestimate the power of white space. It invites the reader to read your résumé—and that's important, considering your résumé gets looked at for an average of seven to ten seconds. If you cram too much in, it will overwhelm the readers, and they will quickly move on to the next résumé in the stack.

3 **BE MINDFUL OF LENGTH.** Your résumé can be longer than one page unless you are a recent graduate. The average résumé is two pages, but your situation may call for three pages. As long as everything on your résumé is relevant to your career, three pages is an acceptable résumé practice.

4 **SAVE REFERENCES FOR ANOTHER DAY.** Never include references as part of your résumé. These should be a separate document and only provided if requested.

5 **CREATE A SOLID HEADING.** Your heading should include your full name, address, phone number, and e-mail address. Don't have a professional e-mail address yet? Register one using your FirstNameLastName@_____.com. Don't for-

get to revisit your voicemail message, too. Make sure your voicemail is professional and clearly states your first name, last name, and how you can be reached.

START WITH THE ACTION, NOT YOURSELF. Whether it's the summary or the body of the résumé, focus on the accomplishments. It may feel weird, but you'll probably end up speaking in the third person.

DO INCLUDE A SUMMARY. A résumé summary is also code for why you're made for the job. This is your chance to tell the reader what you can bring to the table in five to seven sentences. This should include your title, years of experience, core skills, accomplishments, and a few key personality traits. More important, it should speak louder than all of the other résumés in the stack. If you're having a hard time highlighting your key assets, ask your previous boss, your peers, or the people who sit at your table to shed some insight.

LIST YOUR PROFESSIONAL EXPERIENCE. Start with your most recent job first and then work your way back. Make sure to include the following: name of company, title, years worked (no reason to include months), and five to seven accomplishments on the job in bullet form.

INCLUDE YOUR EDUCATION. List your institution name, location, degree, major, and minor. Avoid including a GPA and your graduation date unless you're a recent grad.

VOLUNTEER EXPERIENCE, CLUBS, AND ACTIVITIES: Only include these if they are applicable to the job you are applying for. These can be a great way to highlight some experience you did not get on the job.

SAVE YOUR RÉSUMÉ AS A PDF WHEN EMAILING. This will ensure everyone will be able to open it. Because if they can't open it, they aren't going to read it.

résumé activity

KEY WORDS FOR THE INDUSTRY

WORDS OTHERS WOULD USE TO DESCRIBE YOU

ACTION VERBS

METRICS
(SALES GOALS, MONEY SAVED, ETC.)

MILESTONES

SCOPE

"You can have everything in life you want if you will just help enough other people get what they want."

—Zig Ziglar

chapter 6

The Skinny on LinkedIn

Think a résumé and LinkedIn are the same thing? Think again.

Unlike a résumé, a LinkedIn profile offers you many opportunities to expand on your résumé—including an extra hint at your personality and your network with other professionals. Not to mention, if you're not taking into consideration that some employers may actually prefer to see your LinkedIn over your résumé, you could be seriously missing out on opportunities.

New to the LinkedIn scene? Maybe, maybe not, but things change and rather quickly, so even if you already have a profile you may need a refresher. To get inspiration, take a few minutes and research trending profiles. Here's a little etiquette to help get your profile up to speed.

1 **INCLUDE A PICTURE.** Don't start connecting with people until you have a profile picture of yourself. Unlike your Facebook profile picture with your besties, this should be a professional headshot that features you solo.

2 **KEEP IT PROFESSIONAL.** Unlike other social media platforms, LinkedIn is a business social network. So avoid the urge to talk about anything that isn't relevant to business.

3 **AVOID PROFILE CREEPING.** There's nothing that turns off a potential employer or connection faster than excessive profile stalking. That's right, every time you check someone's LinkedIn profile, they can see it's you. Go there once, write down the information you need and resist double dipping. If the temptation is too great, change your Privacy and Settings manually.

4 **DON'T CONNECT WITH PEOPLE YOU DON'T KNOW.** Forget your high school or college popularity contest. On LinkedIn, it's not about how many connections

you have that matters; it's about the value and relevancy each connection brings. Connect only with people with whom you have a legitimate connection.

5 **PERSONALIZE YOUR WELCOME MESSAGE.** When connecting with someone on LinkedIn, opt out of the default template: "I'd like to add you to my professional network on LinkedIn." Instead, send a personal message to provide the reader with some sort of context of why you should connect.

6 **DISCONNECT FROM NEGATIVE NANCY.** When posting anything on social media, lean toward being positive. The classic, "If you can't say anything nice, then don't say anything at all" still applies.

7 **DON'T LET YOUR PROFILE READ LIKE A RÉSUMÉ.** Resist duplicating your résumé verbatim, and take advantage of the opportunities your LinkedIn profile has to offer. For starters, create a keyword-rich and SEO (Search Engine Optimized) summary. To do this, revisit your career keywords and add them throughout your profile. Don't forget to highlight your extracurricular activities, your volunteer experience, and the causes that you care about. Most importantly, make sure your profile is 100-percent complete.

8 **CHECK BACK FREQUENTLY.** You don't want to ignore your new connections or miss an opportunity to respond or connect.

9 **UPDATE YOUR PRIVACY ON PERSONAL PAGES.** Many of your online profiles are public by default. If you don't want potential employers creeping on your profiles, update your privacy settings. Not sure how to do that? Just ask Google.

10 **AS LONG AS WE'RE BEING SOCIAL . . .** be social on all your favorite sites; Facebook, Twitter, Pinterest, and Google+ are all great places to follow your favorite companies, build your profile, and expand your network. Just be sure to have a plan—social media can monopolize your time if you don't have a system to keep it in check. Add social media maintenance to your calendar, and set a timer to keep your time limited and focused.

"On what high-performing companies should be striving to create: A great place for great people to do great work."

—Marilyn Carlson

chapter 7

Company Hit List

relationships

T his is where it starts to come together: connecting the meaningful relationships you'll be building with the organizations where you would like to work.

But let's not get ahead of ourselves. The first thing you need to do is define the organizations. Think about your values and how they can translate to the specific organizations and their missions. If you value work–life balance and hear stories of an organization that has employees working around the clock, that organization may not be a good fit with your values. Use the space below to write down the values that are important to you in an organization.

What Matters To Me ✎

Next, think about your value system and ask yourself some of the following questions:

Do you want to be a big fish in a small pond or vice versa?

Are you looking to join the corporate world or ride the waves of a start-up?

What sparks excitement in you?

Now file this away for later. It's time to list all of the organizations that get you excited. Go ahead and write them all down in the big yellow boxes below. Don't worry about the two lines quite yet. We'll explain who goes there in chapter 8. If your list is short, you may need to do a little research. Check out your city's top places to work, FORBES hot start-up list, and the Chamber of Commerce; search LinkedIn to get ideas for companies you may not have realized are in your backyard; and don't forget to reach out to the people who sit at your table.

My Company Hit List

IDEO

Jeanette Walker
Dylan Raymond

Next, think about how your value system jives with the organizations listed above. Do you need to cross any off your list?

"Call it a clan, call it a network, call it a tribe, call it a family. Whatever you call it, whoever you are, you need one."

—Jane Howard

chapter 8

Building Meaningful Relationships

M aking professional connections solely online is not the same as building meaningful relationships. Neither is meeting people simply to see what they can do for you.

Much like your personal relationships, building meaningful relationships (otherwise known as networking) takes trust, face time, patience, and commitment. And much like personal relationships that last, professional relationships go both ways. Most importantly, these relationships can ultimately make the difference between landing or not landing the job.

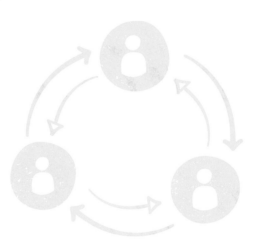

So let's get started. Take ten minutes and write down everyone you know: best friends, casual acquaintances, coworkers, and even Facebook friends. Build from there; just like six degrees of separation, the links are probably closer than you think. Don't include the people who sit at your table. They already made the list. Whether this list is ten people or one hundred, the important thing is now you've got the start of your contact list.

Human Resources

These are individuals who work in HR; they will be plenty knowledgeable when it comes to jobs and résumés, and they may provide some assistance with résumé feedback or job leads.

Inner Circle

These are not only connections you know well but also connections that know what you are capable of making happen. These connections could easily recommend you for your next position, as they are both well-connected and well-versed in your background.

Second Circle

_____

_____

_____

_____

_____

_____

_____

These connections are familiar, but not as well-versed in your skill set or accomplishments as your inner circle. They make damn good cheerleaders, the kind that will work hard to get you connected to other peo-ple in their network.

Third Circle

_____

_____

_____

_____

_____

_____

_____

People in this group may be distant friends or they may be closer friends without a clear understanding of how they can help. This is your opportunity to see who they know.

Once you've identified whom you would like to build meaningful relationships with, it's time to connect them with the organizations you identified earlier in your hit list and start building. Go back to pages 70-75 and fill in the blanks, who do you know where?

Now we're sure you're probably asking yourself, *How do I activate these connections?*

1 **DON'T WASTE YOUR TIME DRINKING WHITE WHEN YOU REALLY WANT RED.** Understand what you need and what you hope to gain. Define your goals for the connection so that you have a guide for your conversation.

2 **ASSESS THE BEST METHOD FOR MAKING THE CONNECTION.** Is the person a close friend you can text directly, or do you need a more formal introduction? The easiest way to make or ask for an introduction is to reach out via e-mail or LinkedIn and simply ask for the introduction or make the introduction on your own. Either way, state your name, a few key points about your background, and what you would like to accomplish. Invite them to join you for a cup of coffee. Be prepared with a few dates and times a week or two out that work for you.

3 **DO YOUR HOMEWORK, AND BE PREPARED FOR THE MEETING.** This meeting should last about thirty minutes; plan for it. Prepare your questions and write them down so you don't forget. Why did you want to meet with this person? Know exactly how they can help, and be prepared to ask for it.

You will need an elevator speech. An elevator speech clearly defines who you are, your professional highlights, and tells the person what you're looking for. Take a minute to jot it down here.

My Elevator Speech

who are
you?

what are your
professional
highlights?

what are you
looking for?

When it comes to your elevator speech, practice makes perfect. Call yourself and leave a voice-mail. How does your elevator speech sound when you play it back?

4 FOLLOW UP A DAY OR TWO BEFORE THE MEETING. Don't ask if it still works for them. Instead let them know how much you are looking forward to meeting them and confirm the day and time.

5 GIVE YOURSELF PLENTY OF TIME TO GET READY ON THE DAY OF THE MEETING. You don't want to be late. It's OK to bring your résumé; just remember that this is not an interview, and it might not be appropriate to bring it out. Let your gut guide you as you have your conversation. You should also be prepared to pay. (If you don't want pay for coffee it's OK to find another meeting place.) You asked for this meeting, so it's only fair, and it's the nice thing to do.

6 ONCE YOU HAVE YOUR COFFEE . . . you may find it difficult to start the conversation in a meaningful and productive way. If you're having problems, try one of the conversation starters on page 87; they go beyond small talk and will help you get to point.

Conversation Starters

"Thank you for meeting with me. I've heard such wonderful things about you and [insert company name]. How long have your worked for [insert company name]?"

"My [insert contact name] mentioned that you recently [insert comment]. How is that going for you?"

"I saw [insert fact] on LinkedIn. That must have been interesting. Can you tell me about it?"

Try to keep the questions open-ended. Questions that begin with who, what, where, when, and how will get the person talking. Questions that can be answered with a simple yes or no will make starting a conversation even more challenging.

REMEMBER TO END ON TIME, FOLLOW UP, AND COMMUNICATE ANY OUTCOMES. Knowing their advice or connection was useful will make them feel good about what they did. So go ahead and spread some joy!

Do your homework **BEFORE** and **AFTER** every meeting. Capture your point-of-contact's contact information and conversation details in one easy-to-access spot. Include the following:

CONTACT NAME

WHAT'S THE CONNECTION? (HOW DO YOU KNOW THEM?)

CONTACT PERSONAL INFORMATION (GET TO KNOW THEM, FAMILY, ETC.)

EMAIL AND PHONE NUMBER

MEETING DATE:

QUESTIONS TO ASK

WHAT DID YOU DISCUSS? (THIS WILL HELP YOU WRITE A PERSONAL THANK-YOU NOTE LATER.)

NEXT STEPS (NEW CONTACTS THEY ARE GOING TO CONNECT YOU WITH)

THANK-YOU CARD OR RESPONSE SENT: _____ DATE: _____

Make it a habit to genuinely check in. Your connections have a lot going on; don't forget to drop a note and touch base on occasion. This will help your relationships last longer and keep you top of mind when opportunities arise.

that this is about

not finding a job immediately.

that lead to a job months later.

"Be so good they can't ignore you."

–Steve Martin

chapter 9

Your Best Interview Yet

People make first impressions in a snap! The minute we meet someone, our brains have ways of interpreting, sensing, and computing every little detail. When you take that into account, you can start to understand why it's so important to take the time to think about what kind of first impression you want to make. From interview prep and your professional appearance to the graceful follow-up, your best interview is just a few goals away.

Interview Prep

Be on time and be prepared. From the time you arrive until you leave, you will have conversations with a variety of individuals at the company. To help prepare for your next interview, it's important to gather insight on the company and the people you will be meeting with along with your introduction, fillers, answers to common interview questions, graceful exit, and the perfect follow-up.

Properly Announce Your Arrival

To properly announce your arrival, introduce yourself, confidently state your name, and tell the person why you're here and who you are meeting. If they come to shake your hand, don't be a limp fish; shake it like you mean it!

Your Fillers

If the person interviewing you is running late, you may need to be prepared to fill ten to fifteen minutes with HR or the receptionist. This can be a delicate situation and will most likely require you to pay close attention to their cues. No matter what you do, stray from potentially loaded conversations, politics, and current events. Instead, comment on the beautiful space, location, or popular restaurants in the area.

Question and Answer Prep

Prep can go a long way when it comes to off-the-cuff interview questions and answers. To get into interview mode, try answering some of the questions below.

Can you tell me a little bit about yourself?

Provide a brief overview of your work highlights. This is your elevator speech. It should be thirty to sixty seconds long. Focus on professional highlights, who you are, and what you do.

What do you know about the company?

Hopefully you did your research! Make sure to check the news before you go; you never know what company developments may be covered. Provide a quote from this morning's paper.

Why do you want this job?

Focus on why you like the company. Think about the products or the services they offer and why you're excited about them. Connect their offerings back to your experience.

What are your strengths / weaknesses

The point of this question is often debated, but it does get asked. Tell them what you do well (this should be easy if you're familiar with your accomplishments). Tell a story about your weakness and how you continue to learn and challenge yourself.

Share a challenge or conflict you recently faced and how you dealt with it.

Pick your favorite accomplishment, and tell the story, the situation, and the outcome.

Where do you see yourself in five years?

Share a few of your career goals, but do not under any circumstances tell them that you want to be in their desk.

What are you looking for in terms of career development?

Be honest about your goals. Revisit Chapter 2 for a quick refresher.

What salary are you seeking?

Have a range. You should know your value, and if you don't, you didn't do your research. But before you go there, try to turn it and have them provide you with a range first.

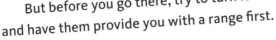

Dressing for the Job

When it comes to an interview, dressing for the job couldn't be more important. Here are a few key points to follow.

- Whatever you do, remember that the day before or of the interview is not the time to play around with a new hairstyle. Instead, keep it simple, clean, and professional.
- Get a manicure. After all, you will be shaking hands a lot.
- Ditch the strong perfumes. Oftentimes, it can easily overwhelm and offend.
- Do wear deodorant. (We had to say it.)
- Make sure your clothes fit you ahead of time. If your pants or blouse are too tight, you will fidget and people will notice. This is uncomfortable for everyone.

Don't have an outfit ready yet? Start with the basic staples below. You might not always like the rules, but you'll have to play by them to get where you want to go. Here are a few key reminders:

- A dress or a blouse with a skirt or dress pants is always a good staple outfit.
- Only wear a skirt or dress if it hits the knee, and pair it with a sweater or blazer.
- Everything should be pressed and free of wrinkles.
- Accessories should be kept to a minimum. Too many jingly bangles or large rings can be distracting.
- Wear cute but comfortable shoes for your style. If you're used to walking in heels, wear them; if not, opt in for a pair of nice flats. Don't go for a pair of six-inch stilettos if "Material Girl" by Madonna was topping the charts the last time you adorned your feet with a pair of heels.

During the Interview

As you're doing all the talking, don't forget to pay attention to what your body is saying. Stand straight and sit up straight—no slouching. Make eye contact. Be warm and genuinely personable but not too loud or gregarious.

Graceful Exit

Before the interview wraps up, ask about the next steps in the process. After you've had that conversation, gather your items, shake the interviewer's hand, and proceed with confidence—no matter how you feel the interview went. Sometimes, the last impression can be just as powerful as the first.

Don't forget to write a brief thank-you note or e-mail, depending on company culture, nonchalantly reiterating why you're perfect for this role and the respect you have for the company.

Hello (Insert name here...)

Thanks again for meeting with me today. I really enjoyed our conversation and appreciate your time and consideration.

After speaking with you, I believe that my experience and accomplishments would be a great fit for (insert role here).

If you have any additional questions please don't hesitate to contact me.

Warm regards,

(Your name...)

"Budgets are actually pretty easy, and budgets are awesome. A budget will buy you a new car. A budget enables you to take that trip to Paris.
A budget helps you to accomplish your life goals and works better than medication for reducing stress and getting a restful night's sleep."

chapter 10

Budget Like A Boss

ost people don't want to sit down and define a budget, let alone stick to one. Now is the time to break up with that notion once and for all. Whether you're considering a career change or you've just been laid off, figuring out what you can and can't survive without will be key in coming up with a budget that allows you flexibility to achieve your gōls.

Just fill out the table below with your budget amount and actual bill.

DESCRIPTION	BUDGET	ACTUAL
CAR		
MONTHLY PAYMENT		
INSURANCE		
GASOLINE		
FOOD		
GROCERY STORE		
LIQUOR STORE		
HOME		
MORTGAGE | RENT		
UTILITIES (ELECTRIC, HEAT, WATER, AND GARBAGE)		
INSURANCE		
HOME IMPROVEMENT SERVICES		
OTHER HOME LOANS		
WIRELESS SERVICE		
HOME ENTERTAINMENT (CABLE TELEVISION, STREAMING SERVICE)		
CELL PHONES		

DESCRIPTION	BUDGET	ACTUAL
APPEARANCE		
CLOTHING STORES		
DRY CLEANING		
HAIRCUT		
MAKEUP		
NAILS		
ENTERTAINMENT		
RESTAURANTS		
ACTIVITIES		
TRAVEL		
HEALTH INSURANCE		
HEALTH-CARE BILLS		
LIFE INSURANCE		
GIFTS		
FAMILY BIRTHDAYS		
FRIENDS' BIRTHDAYS		
HOLIDAYS		
FITNESS		
COLLEGE SAVINGS		

DESCRIPTION	BUDGET	ACTUAL
TOTAL EXPENSES		
TOTAL INCOME		
DIFFERENCE		

Now, be ruthlessly realistic: from the list above, what can you live without? Starbucks lattes? Finishing the yard? Your favorite sushi happy hour you've been talking about nonstop? Just remember, the sacrifice doesn't have to be forever.

"The most effective way to do it, is to do it."

–Amelia Earhart

chapter 11

Keep Calm
and
Focus on
Your Gōl

Congratulations! We told you at the start this wouldn't be easy; we knew it would take a lot of time and effort on your part to get this far. So why not take a moment to make sure you completed Gōl's to-do list? If you can check everything off, give yourself a pat on the back, pour yourself that glass of wine, or buy yourself those shoes (assuming there's room in your budget). After all, you deserve it! Keep in mind this is a living and breathing list, one that needs to be revisited often to stay relevant in today's modern world.

When you get the call, don't forget to share what you've learned—pay it forward!

Have you defined what your life tomorrow will look like?

Have you set professional and personal goals?

Have you maintained a to-do list to keep you motivated?

Have you defined who will sit at your table?

Have you completed your résumé?

Are you on LinkedIn?

Do you have a company hit list?

Have you started making meaningful connections?

Are you taking notes?

Are you prepared to interview?

Have you set a budget?

Are you ready for your next adventure?

chapter 12

Keeping it all Together

Writing things down is something we highly encourage. We hope you've enjoyed taking the time to step away from your device, reflect, and commit your job-search goals to paper. As you start and continue your journey, use the following calendar to help you stay organized and track your goals, interviews, networking events, and those inevitable wine nights and celebrations with your girlfriends.

month: year:

SUNDAY	MONDAY	TUESDAY	WEDNESDAY

notes

to do

month:		year:	
SUNDAY	MONDAY	TUESDAY	WEDNESDAY

notes ————————————————————————————
————————————————————————————————————
————————————————————————————————————
————————————————————————————————————

THURSDAY	FRIDAY	SATURDAY

to do

month: year:

SUNDAY	MONDAY	TUESDAY	WEDNESDAY

notes

THURSDAY	FRIDAY	SATURDAY

to do

month: year:

SUNDAY	MONDAY	TUESDAY	WEDNESDAY

notes _____
_____
_____
_____

to do

month: year:

SUNDAY	MONDAY	TUESDAY	WEDNESDAY

notes _____

_____

_____

_____

THURSDAY	FRIDAY	SATURDAY

to do

month: year:

SUNDAY	MONDAY	TUESDAY	WEDNESDAY

notes _____
_____
_____
_____

THURSDAY	FRIDAY	SATURDAY

to do

month: year:

SUNDAY	MONDAY	TUESDAY	WEDNESDAY

notes _____
_____
_____
_____

THURSDAY	FRIDAY	SATURDAY

to do

month: year:

SUNDAY	MONDAY	TUESDAY	WEDNESDAY

notes _____
_____
_____
_____

THURSDAY	FRIDAY	SATURDAY

to do

month: year:

SUNDAY	MONDAY	TUESDAY	WEDNESDAY

notes

to do

month: **year:**

SUNDAY	MONDAY	TUESDAY	WEDNESDAY

notes _____

to do

month: year:

SUNDAY	MONDAY	TUESDAY	WEDNESDAY

notes

THURSDAY	FRIDAY	SATURDAY

to do

About the Authors

KATHY ENGEN

Kathy grew up in a small town surrounded by a loving family; she learned that life wasn't always easy or fair but to always do the very best with what she had. Kathy graduated from St. Cloud State University with a BS in speech communications and has been in motion ever since. She's held a variety of roles throughout her career: a recruiter, a trainer, a career coach, a stay-at-home mom, and most recently, a realtor, so she knows a thing or two about the job search. In addition to navigating her own job search, Kathy has assisted hiring managers in reviewing résumés and making hiring decisions, led workshops on a variety of job-search topics, and coached hundreds of others in achieving their career goals. She's a self-driven person who's not afraid of change. She has always believed that everyone has something to offer and that the right job is there—you just need to know how to find it. When Kathy's not working you can find her at home trying to keep it all together, carving out time for her family and friends, or enjoying a good meal with a big glass of wine.

LINDA HEATH

A native of Tucson, Linda fled to a cooler climate, settling down in Minneapolis, Minnesota, where she found her passion in marketing and advertising. She spent many years strategizing away at ad agencies, in retail marketing and health care. When she was laid off, she went to work finding a job with the same gusto she once used when traveling and discovering a special place off the beaten path. Her methods landed her in a great new job. With many friends looking for "what's next," Linda found herself doling out a lot of sage advice. When she saw her pals were finding jobs using her tips, Linda realized there was an opportunity to connect all these dots.

When she is not helping people get connected, you can find Linda dreaming about her next adventure with her family.